What's Normal?

Written by
Joanne Good

Illustrated by
Ana Sánchez

Edited by
Suzanne Mamo

Cover and additional design by
Ana Sánchez

Editing by Suzanne Mamo

No part of this publication may be reproduced, stored in a retrieval system, or transmitted in any form or by any means, electronic, mechanical, photocopying, recording or otherwise, without written permission of the publisher. For information regarding permission, send an email to joanneggood@gmail.com. This edition first published in Ontario Canada in 2023 by Joanne Good.

ISBN 978-1-7390343-0-6

Copyright © 2023, by Joanne Good. All rights reserved.

Dedicated to
Zachary and Joshua

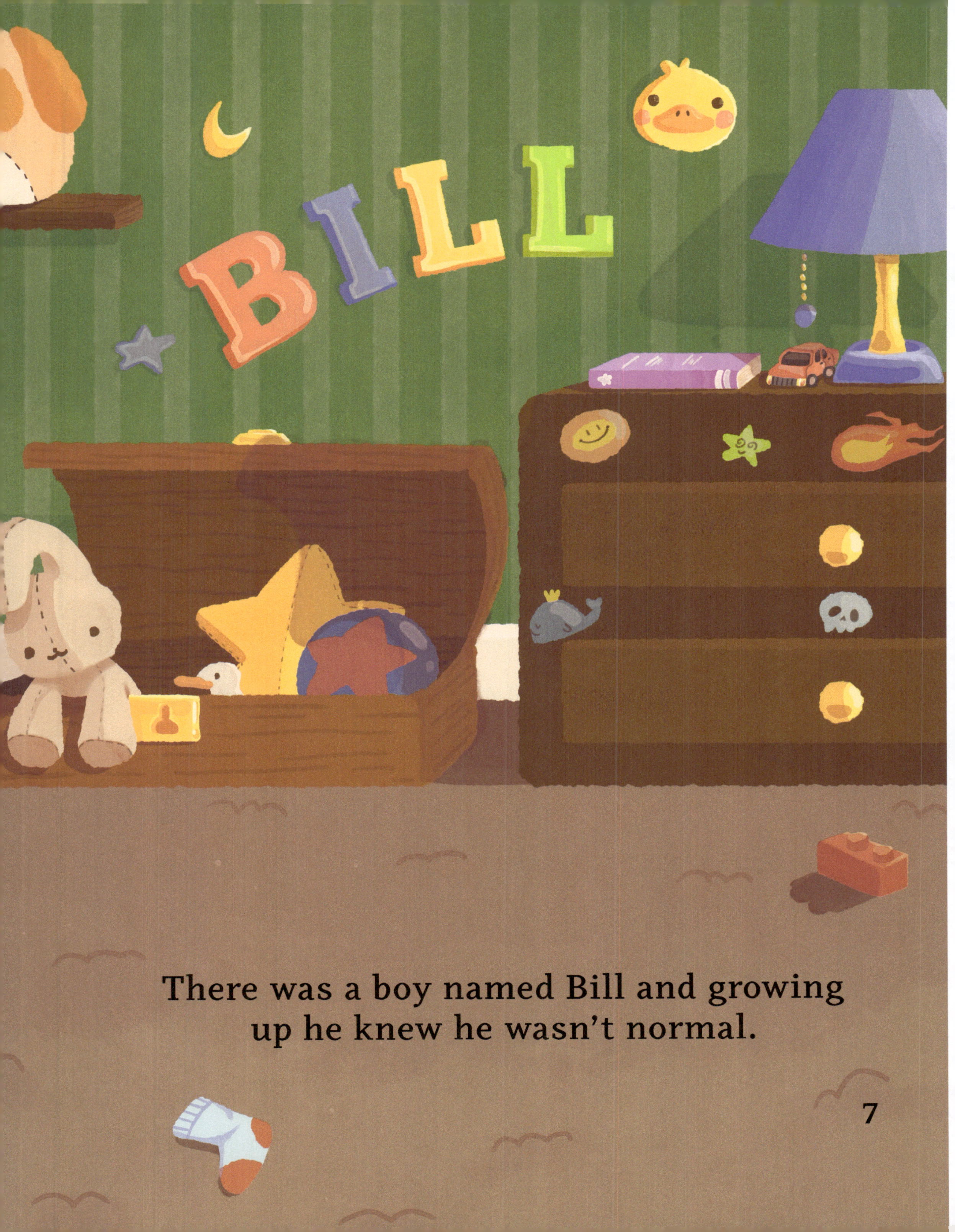

There was a boy named Bill and growing up he knew he wasn't normal.

Every time he went swimming, he didn't want to take off his shoes. Everyone would stare and laugh at him.

His Mom always said "Don't be embarrassed by them, you were born that way for a reason".

As Bill grew up he learned to hide his feet from people until one day during high school he had to take swimming in gym.

The swimming coach noticed his feet right away and pulled him aside.

After a few swim classes the coach talked Bill into joining the school swim team.

Bill was winning every match he competed in. He was swimming faster than everyone else.

After a few years of competing in different swim competitions he caught the eye of a scout for the Canadian swim team.

He approached Bill and recruited him.

Bill was so excited he ran home. He told his Mom she was right after all these years. His feet were special, he didn't have to be embarrassed anymore.

He was proud to have feet like a duck! Bill was chosen to represent his country on the world's competitive swim team.

She said, "I told you so. You have a special gift, God blessed you with your feet".

At that moment Bill finally understood his purpose in life — to become a competitive swimmer and to represent his country.

It wasn't easy. Bill had to work hard, harder than he ever did in his life. But he strongly felt it was worth everything.

Bill went on to compete internationally and won the gold several times. He won his races by a mile. He was the fastest swimmer in history.

Even the previous gold medalist couldn't believe how fast a swimmer Bill was. Bill was able to hold his title for many years.

As Bill got older, he retired from the Canadian swim team.

With his swimming talent and success, Bill decided to coach younger kids to become the next competitive swimmers.

During his lessons, Bill would tell his students his story of how he was embarrassed by being different.

Bill told his students they should never make fun of someone because they're different.

He explained those who are different can use their miracles to achieve amazing things in life.

The students laughed, but in a serious tone, he said he got the last laugh.

He made the Canadian swim team and throughout his swimming career won several metals and awards.

Just ask Bill himself, he was the perfect example.

www.ingramcontent.com/pod-product-compliance
Lightning Source LLC
Chambersburg PA
CBHW042248100526
44587CB00002B/66